Toward a Healthy Tomorrow

How to: Find a Friend for me! It's you

Toward a Healthy Tomorrow

How to: Find a Friend for me! It's you

Lowell E. White Jr., MD

Order this book online at www.trafford.com
or email orders@trafford.com

Most Trafford titles are also available at major online book retailers.

Printed in the United States of America.

ISBN: 978-1-4269-5293-7 (sc)
ISBN: 978-1-4269-5294-4 (e)

Trafford rev. 01/07/2011

 www.trafford.com

North America & International
toll-free: 1 888 232 4444 (USA & Canada)
phone: 250 383 6864 ♦ fax: 812 355 4082

Preface

There is no question about our fiscal, social and biological problems with Health in the United States and the World. Other than Physicians and Surgeons there are three additional players in the "health care" game: drug and instrument companies, insurance companies and hospitals in general (both for profit and not for profit). The latter three tend to interfere with Dr- Patient relationships. Specialization in Medicine has made General Medicine, Surgery or Psychiatry a thing of the past. In this regard Pediatrics (child care) remains general with many specialties tagged on; Family and Sports Medicine practitioners are limited in number. This makes it difficult for the average healthy individual to identify a Primary Health Care Physician and Surgeon. They usually have to deal with what today we call a Physician's Assistant. Realistically, Health is a personal problem all others can do is: help us to preserve it. Today most advertising and marketing in the Media and Hospitals make disease a commodity with which Health Care can barter.

With the development of Emergency Rooms many clinics have started to call themselves Wellness Clinics to combat this growing trend to capitalize disease. Metaphors are not the answer to the problem and Health has no antonym as History has no sin. The learned professions Medicine, Law and Clergy, with essentially the same Professional Ethics, are the harbingers of Health. The only way this can be directed toward the public is through Education K-12, with Family (jointed or disjointed) understanding. What Universities do with Health is an Academic matter.

Environmentally, there are only three things that interfere with consciousness: 1. Sleep, 2. Acceleration, positive and negative and

3.Oxygen lack; the remaining social insult is poisons. Yes, trauma in the world today is our worst illness. But, it is possible Surgically to fight fire with fire.

Socially, language usage, political and media communication modify with metaphors the way we look at the world and our Health. The disease care systems publicly generated should be not for profit. There is no personal association between Health and Disease (well or sick), only a Public one. The Public Health as a bond is defined by life versus death... Thus, the metaphoric relationship: patient care::health care. Professional Public Health assistance in this arena of "health care" is the responsibility of Medicine, Law and Clergy.

With our sophisticated and advanced form of Medical Care we must accept these truisms. Recognize that the individual understands his or her Health. Our role as a people is to help and not hinder. Things change with generations, interpretation of words and meaning vary. A good example is the metaphor prevalent today "Cool", connoting by many: Ok, Great or Lovely!

Many of the provocative answers may be found in Viking Poetry where expansion of Justice amplifies the Virtue. The word is Ombudsman. Social and Political understanding is Prudent.

Dedicated to Dr Brad Shoup who was there when I needed him, the Class of 1953 School of Medicine and the Class of 1950 College of Pharmacy, University of Washington, Seattle, WA

Thanks:

    To my Editors: Richard Berggren and William Shertzer

    To my Family for being there for me

CONTENTS

*

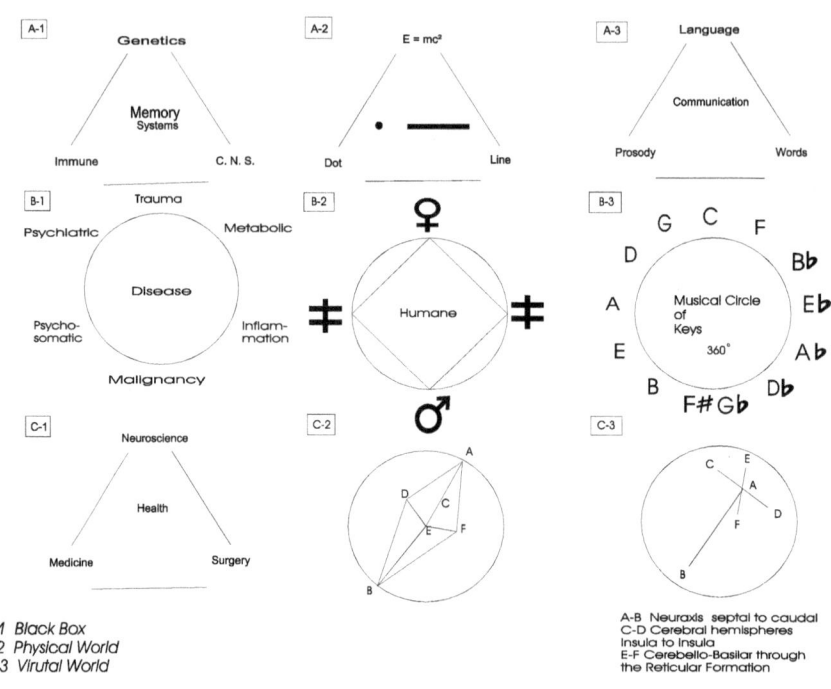

A1 Black Box
B2 Physical World
C3 Virutal World

A-B Neuraxis septal to caudal
C-D Cerebral hemispheres
Insula to Insula
E-F Cerebello-Basilar through
the Reticular Formation

Modeling Examples

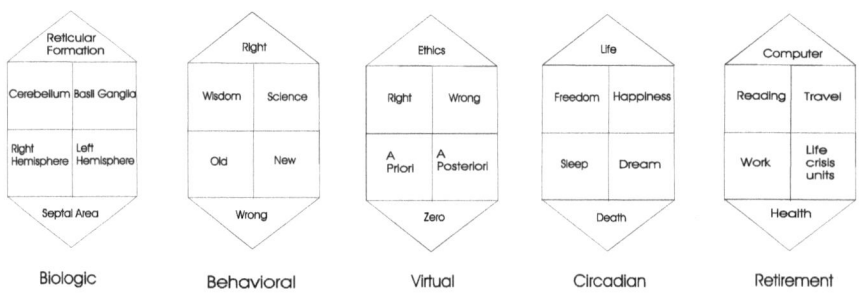

Biologic   Behavioral   Virtual   Circadian   Retirement

Introduction

As a Medical Educator, Neuroscientist and Surgical Neurologist I am impressed by the gender gap and how much I have learned from my students. Further how they respond to mathematics, language and pictures. This is in contrast to the written word which only serves as a template for learning.

For this reason I present these observations in prose, poetry and graphics: The prose to introduce the subject matter, the poetry to address personal responsibility for your Health and the graphics to encourage the reader to think about the subject of the poem in a conceptual fashion.

There is a chicken and the egg problem with the subject matter; polar relations are necessary. A simple Tick-Tack-Toe diagram directed toward the male and the female graphically illustrates the issues and their interrelationships. A model for how we may structure our thinking. Only you the reader can solve this game, using the pyramidal matrix to a personal conclusion*. In your mind you must come to grips with the prime social issues. Be constantly cognizant of the individual's role in his or her Health. What comes first in our thinking, mathematics or language? Undoubtedly how we think: with both! Genetics carries us forward as we have learned to share our feelings with others in an analytical way.

For those who wish to explore this question further in their own thinking I would suggest three books , two old and one new**. But, as you peruse these poems keep in mind: only three biologic organisms stand erect on this planet: trees, humans and penguins. I wish you good speed.

If you feel tempted, I leave you to explore the poems and for the exploration I give you a simple template. This template expands to the simple Tick-Tack-Toe Template of ancient games. Whether this is both an analytical matrix in biology and behavior remains to be seen.

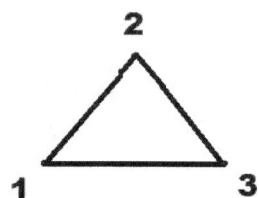

---

*

Reprinted from Society for Neuroscience Poster by Lowell E White Jr, History and Teaching, New Orleans, La 2003 (24.12)

**

Weiner, Norbert, "The Human Use of Human beings", Houghton Mittin Co. Boston, 1950

Edelman, G. H. and Mountcastle, V. B., "The Mindful Brain", MIT Press, Cambridge, 1978

O'Shea, Donal, "The Poincare' Conjecture", Walker Publishing Company, N.Y., 2007

Toward a Healthy Tomorrow

How to: Find a Friend for me! It's you

Concept

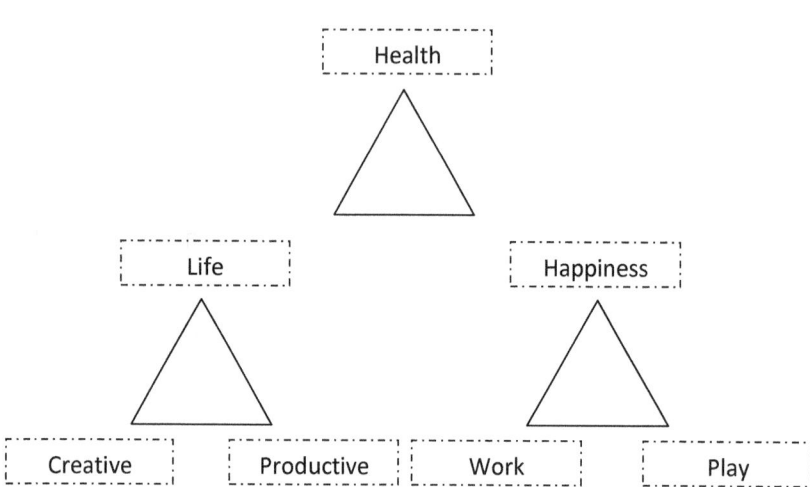

Matrix

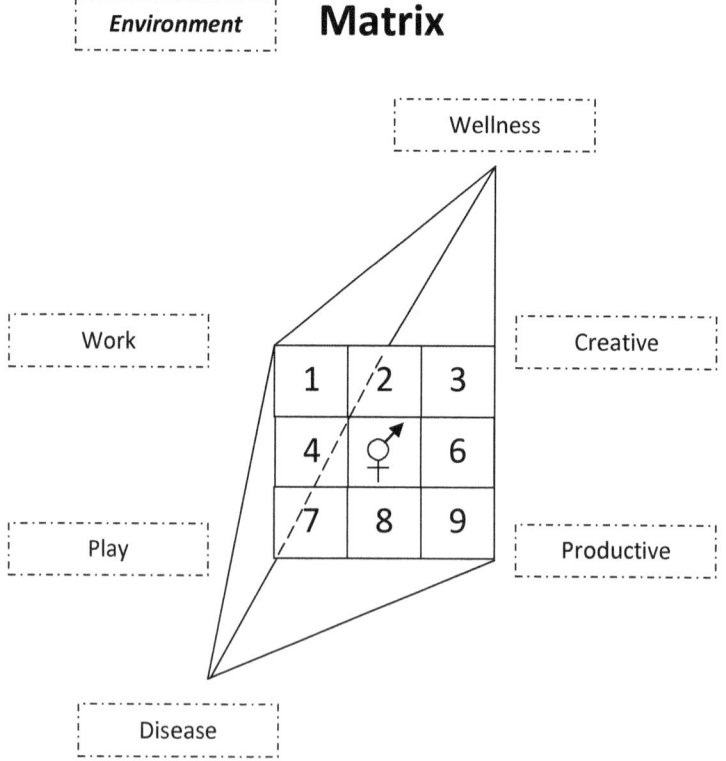

This is Your Health

Health, a gift of nature bestowed on every life
A metaphor for every future
The answer to a prayer: in all Religions
The responsibility first with mother and father with a tool
The sheer pleasure of Health
Let no one put asunder

Passed like a torch to each one of us
Pick it up it's just one of a kind
Remember to bless the one who sneezes
A timely human Health lapse
Not disease but a simple personal seizure
Let justice prevail

Respect your primary Doctor as though a quarterback and friend
Accept help but deny coercion when tendered
It's your Health to preserve, for
Ill Health is not an unjust attitude: disease is here to stay
You have the where with all to recycle" it" with simple hope
The hopeful guide and forceful lamp of Florence Nightingale

Listen each day to the little voice within
Keep in close touch with your own me
To gain a hold on Health is a fertile task
Recharge your Health with accomplishment
Create a happy day: with work as well as play
It is not to win the game, but to be proud of how you play

When the time is right
There is no sin in history
Justice will take its tole
Be resigned to all of this
Wrap your Healthy shroud around you
Lie down to pleasant dreams

PATIENT HEALTH

TRILOGY

(Dr: a salutation for a learned person)

Concept

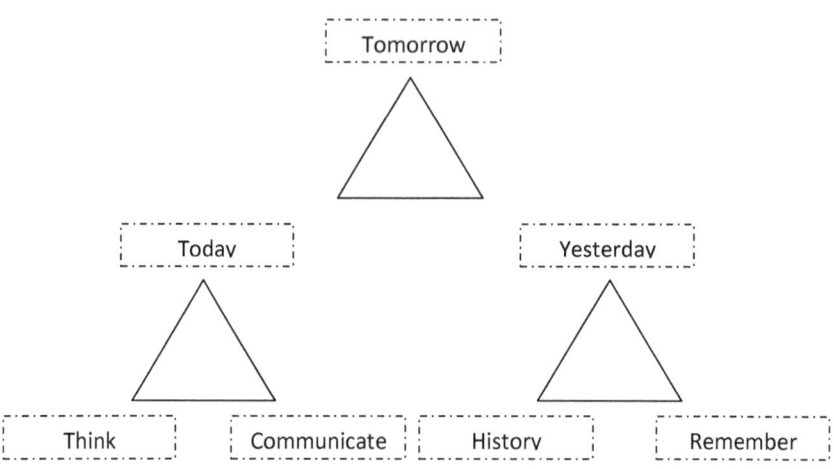

Time **Matrix**

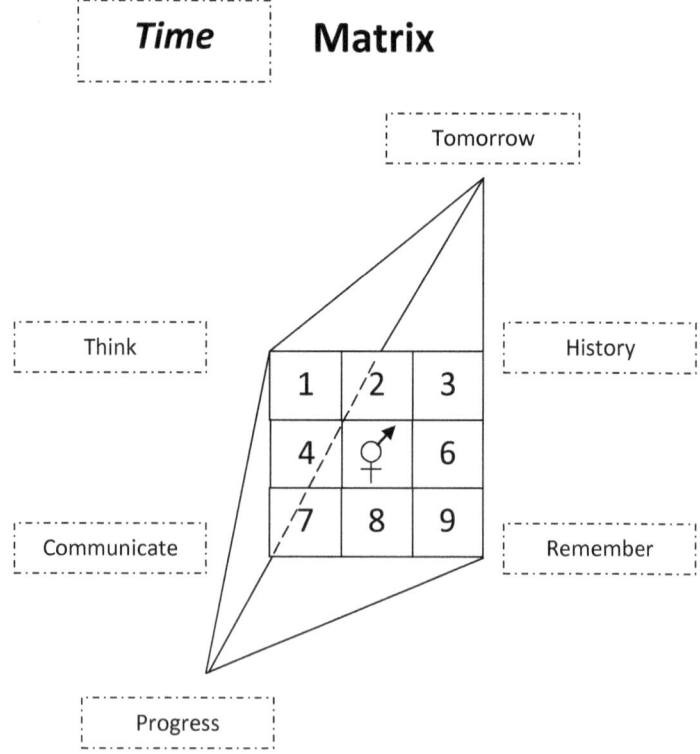

TOMORROW

(Don't let the Dr Make you sick)

Time will tell
When we cross the bar!
Only Mother Nature holds the reins for us
Behold her individual teaching
She holds a trump
A Vicious tool
Control of the Biologic databases
These are three in number:
First our immune system to fight disease
Second our genes that make us what we are
Third our C (entral) N (ervous) S (ystem) or me
Through our CNS we interpret our databases
Thinking, the most primitive form of interpretation
Knowing who we are!

Concept

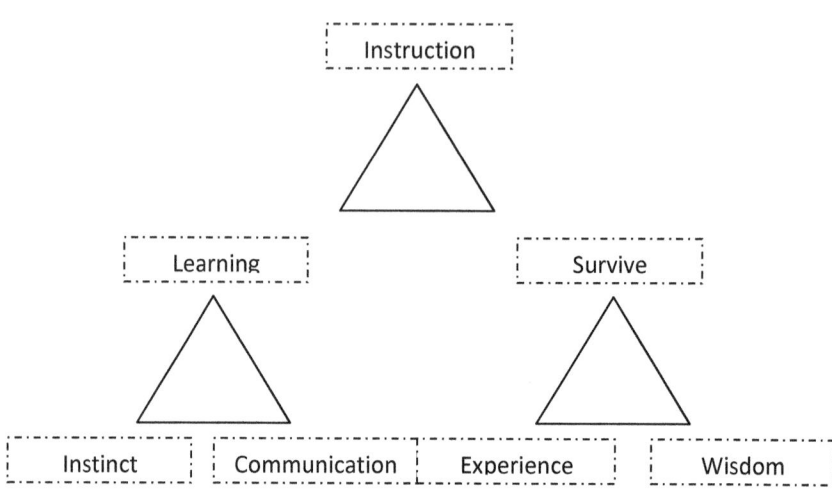

Progress Matrix

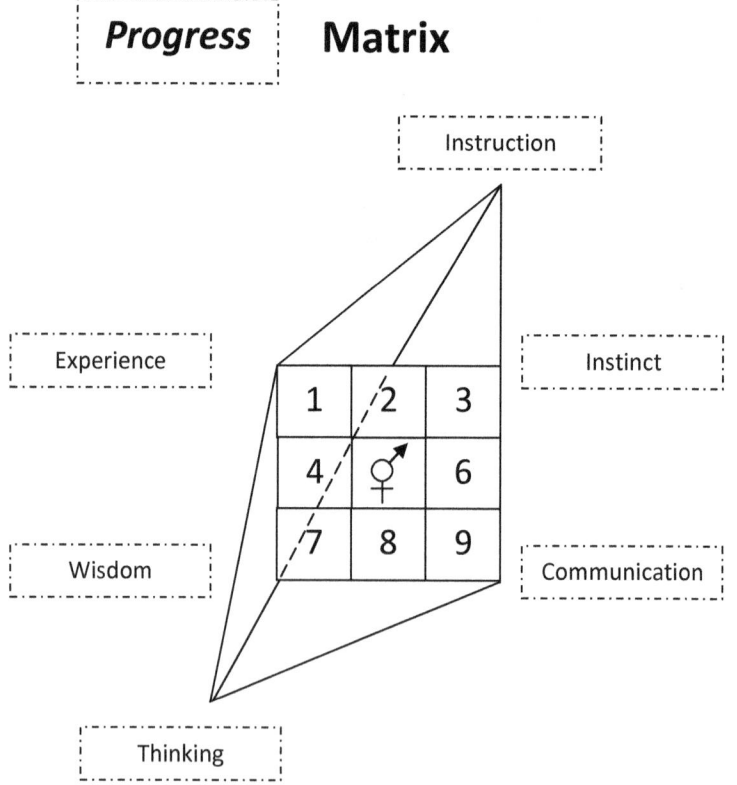

Instruction

(For you and only you)

Remember as you sail

Hoist a Healthy bowsprit

Trust your instincts

And sail a steady course

If the prevailing wind

Does not seem right

To you and yours

Set a new coarse

Find a new confidant, a friend

Concept

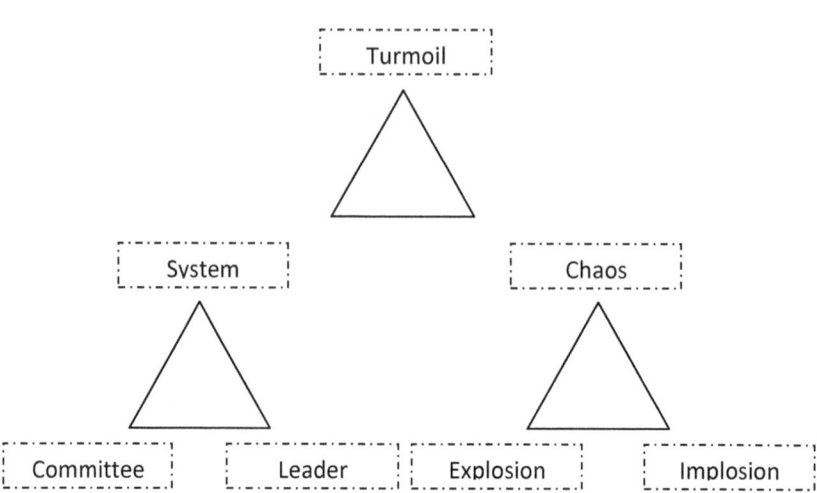

Group Matrix

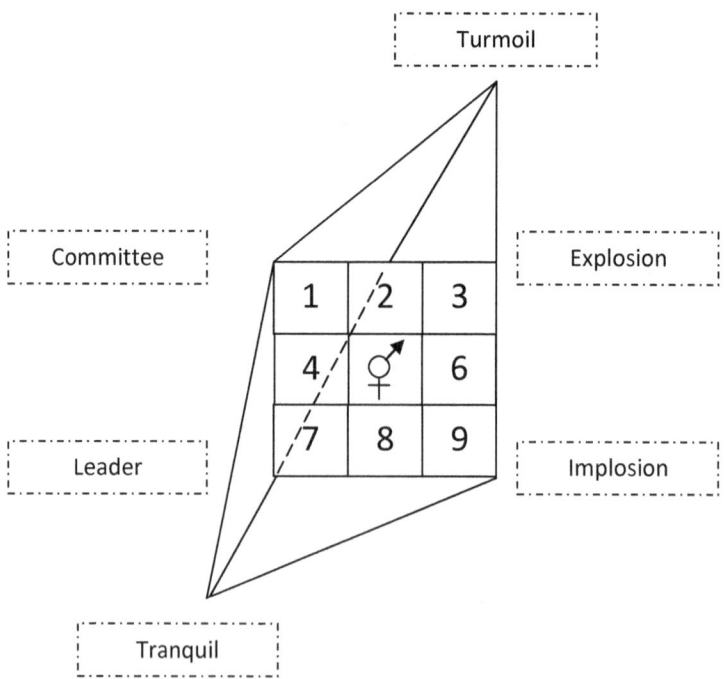

Turmoil

(The ultimate decision)

Progress is:

A two edged sword

It guides us

Toward and in our life

Never waiver in your desire

Health in all its aspects.

When the system fails

Seek a friend: a Health Ombudsman

What is a friend?

Today it is a Primary Physician and Surgeon

A confidant a Quarterback

Primary Friend, Chairman of the committee

Lowell E. White Jr., MD

ETHICAL

TRILOGY

(The way you look at it)

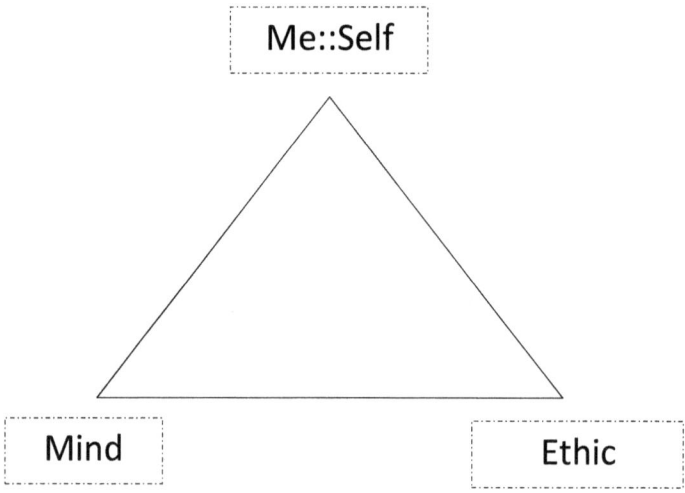

Medifors

What is a metaphor?
      A word for hidden gain?
Law, Medicine, Clergy
      The harbingers of Health

Language how we communicate?
      Written words for Documentation
How to use words?
      Oh! Be discreet

The Nobel powder bowl for War and Peace
      A hidden receptacle for greed
Avoid? Be Prudent
      But do not overfill

Knowledge is Science
      As the Male is Female
Vive La Difference
      As Epilepsy is a Sneeze

Humans like other animals
      Think with lightning speed
Personal, Emotional beauty
      The 4th dimension of life

Winning and Playing
      Life is as a game
It matters not the outcome
      It's how you Play!

Humane Understanding, the only Ethic!
      Stand up for what you believe
For a Cultural Shroud can cover Truth!
      Your Ethic will answer all for you!

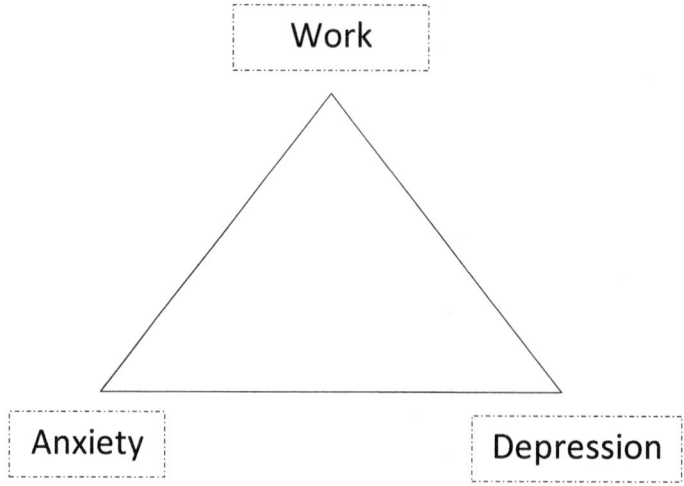

WORK

What is work?
A productive requirement of life,
Productive in a personal sense with Time!
Interrupted by going to the Toilet

Everyone is productive!
Creativity is the personal drive.
Be Humane in all endeavors!
And cross the Bar for you.

You are not alone on the mountain top!
For others gaze upon the theme
Productivity is the name of the game!
Protect your Ethic at all cost.

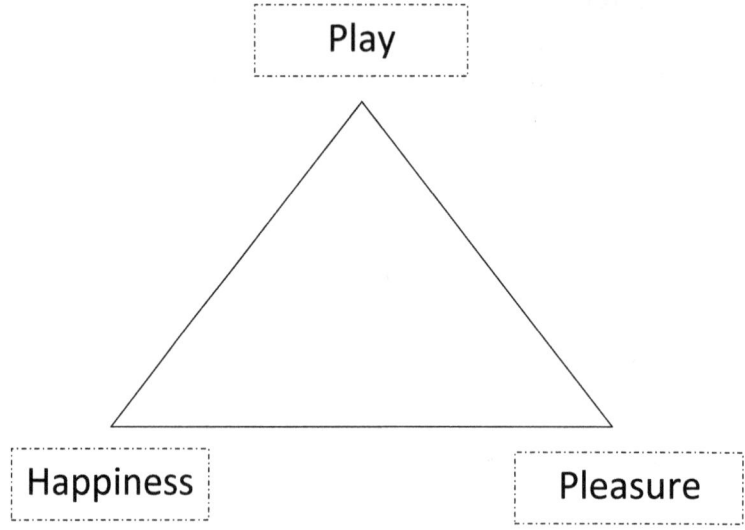

PLAY

What is play?
>A simple outlet for anxiety
To avoid this axiom
>The road to depression!

Do not gamble with your partner!
>It eliminates the truth.
Be forthright and attentive
>And call a Spade a Spade.

Remember there is always time to play
>Though the outcome may be dim
For the way you play
>Protects your Ethic forever!

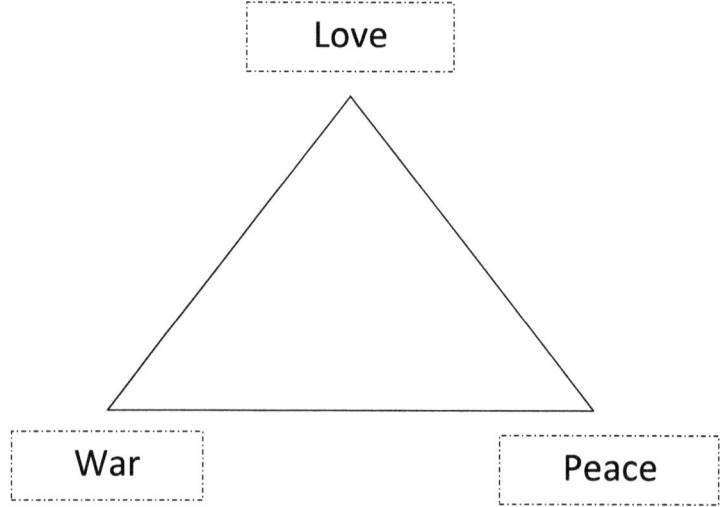

WISDOM

TRILOGY

(Social Service for the Disabled)

Concept

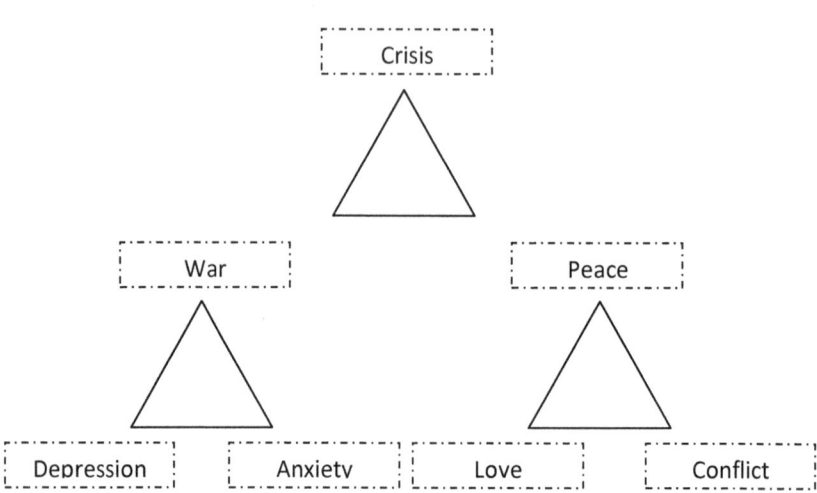

Matrix

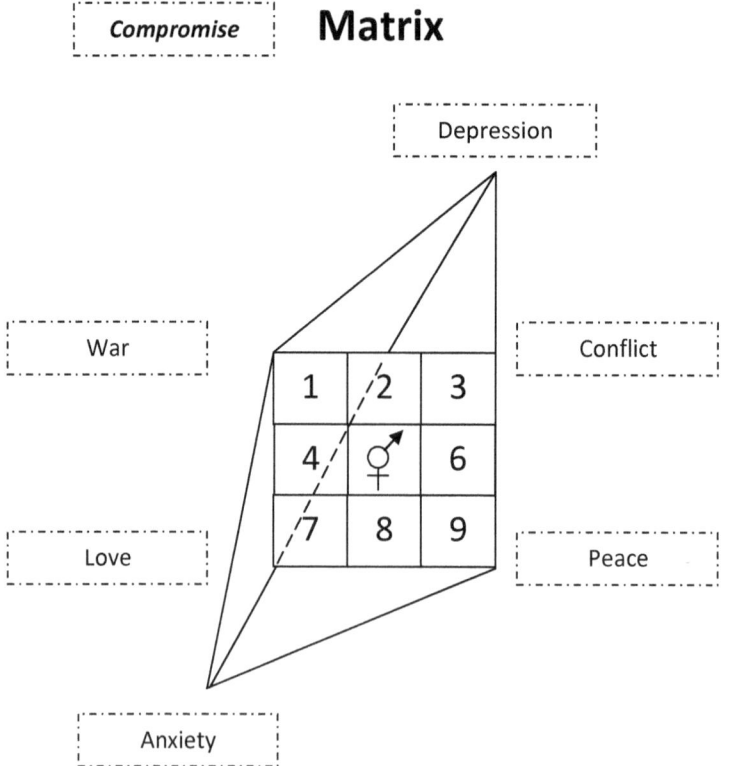

Crisis

Why Armageddon? The end of life!

No, Love is the answer, my human helper

Love is a polar term a driver for human progress

It resides between the givens: War and Peace

The biologic terms are man and woman

Subjected to the raging hormones

In social terms to hunt or gather

What better way to propagate the species

The contradiction to these polar terms

Striving to win driven by hormonal anxiety and social greed

Is to win to live? Driven by others left behind? Or just a sport!

Progress needs it overall and the sun "will" rise

Yes, Art of progress big or small

Requires compromise, harmony and concordance

Through right and wrong we can get along

Building a loving bridge of empathy

Entrusted to climax and compromise

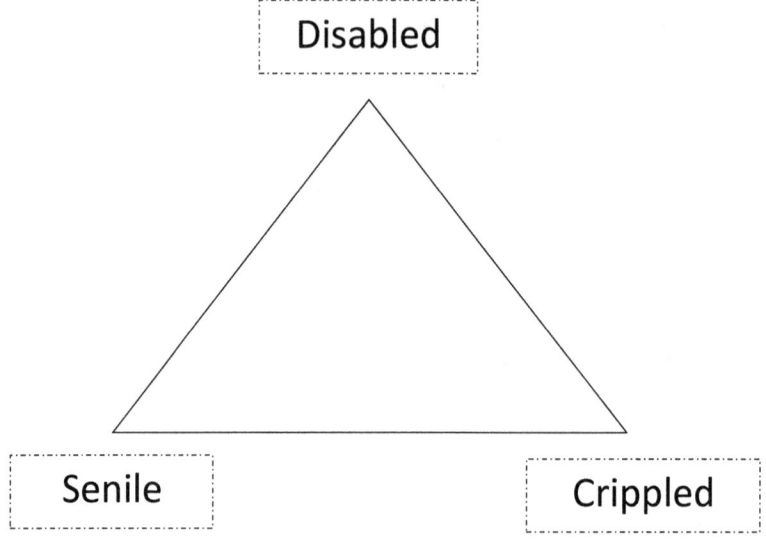

Assisted Living

Are they disabled?

    The senior citizens

Or just our Social detritus

    Is Senility wrong?

A Social question of import

    Alzheimerize or Mesmerize?

What's in a name?

    Like a rose it's a rose

A debatable question for the Politic

    Can they solve this?

Please leave room

    For Epilepsy, Sleep Disorders and Mental Illness

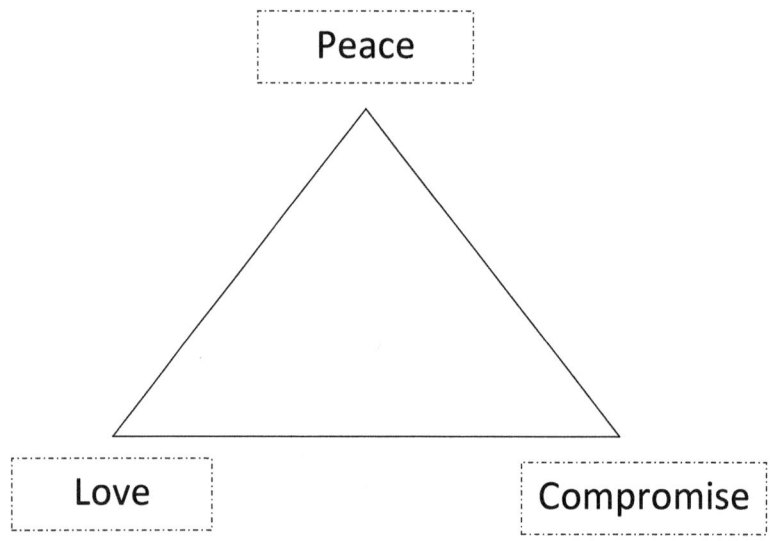

Social Conflict

What are the elements of terror?

Only three in number

Digest their meaning?

Ingest their truth

One can explode

Another can implode

Nobel saw the light

He named it The Peace Prize

Never let your Ethic waver

Protect your fellow "man"

In other words

Remain Humane

Concept

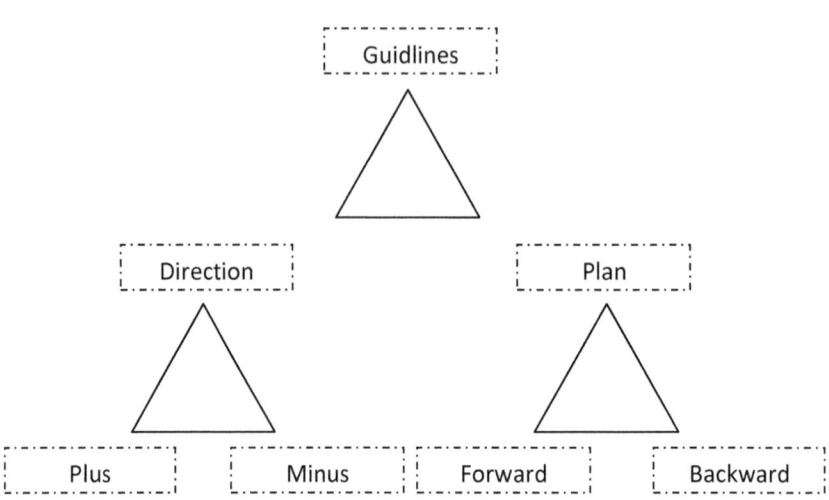

Planning Matrix

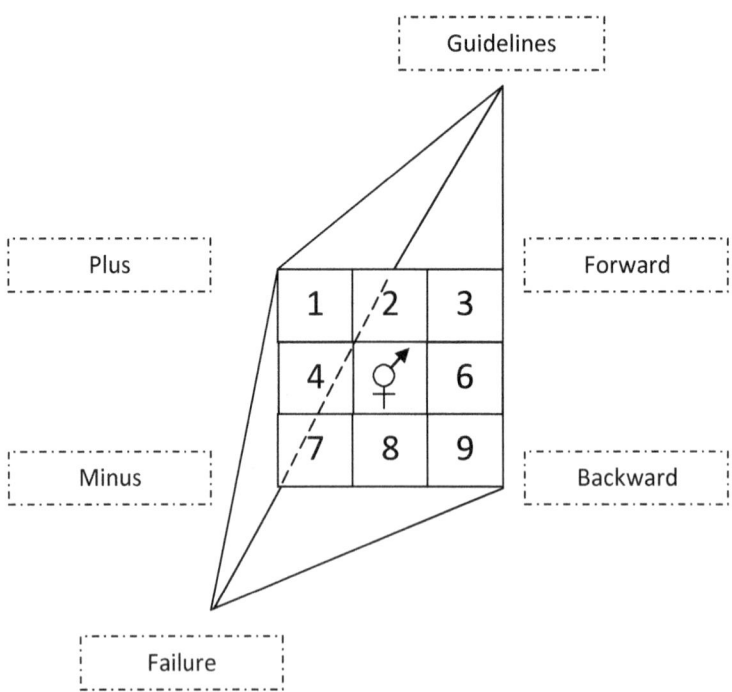

Guidelines

(A search for me)

Take a look at your Health

Is it in a shambles?

Or are your goals being achieved.

Look for alternatives

Are they there?

Remember you are in control

And only need assistance

A friend not a committee to help you

Toward control of Your Health Databases

Three in number!

For this control there is no substitute

The confidant is not defined by politics

Nor dictated by Medicaid or Medicare

The confidant is an Ombudsman

A friend just for you

How do I find the person?

The personal Ombudsman

The Physician Surgeon Psychiatrist of the Committee

Travel far and wide

But, trust your instincts

When help is needed gather it

When the crisis clears be General of Your Health

For the sick-well decision when needed

I sought a friend

Seek your Health Care Ombudsman

Concept

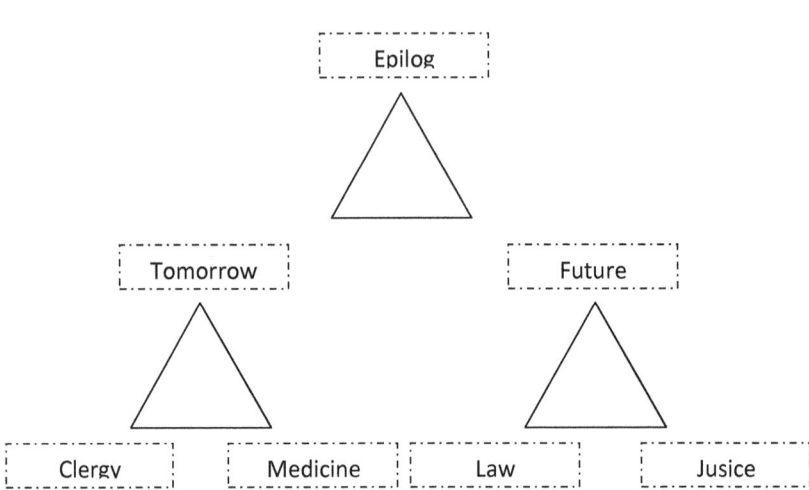

Educational Matrix

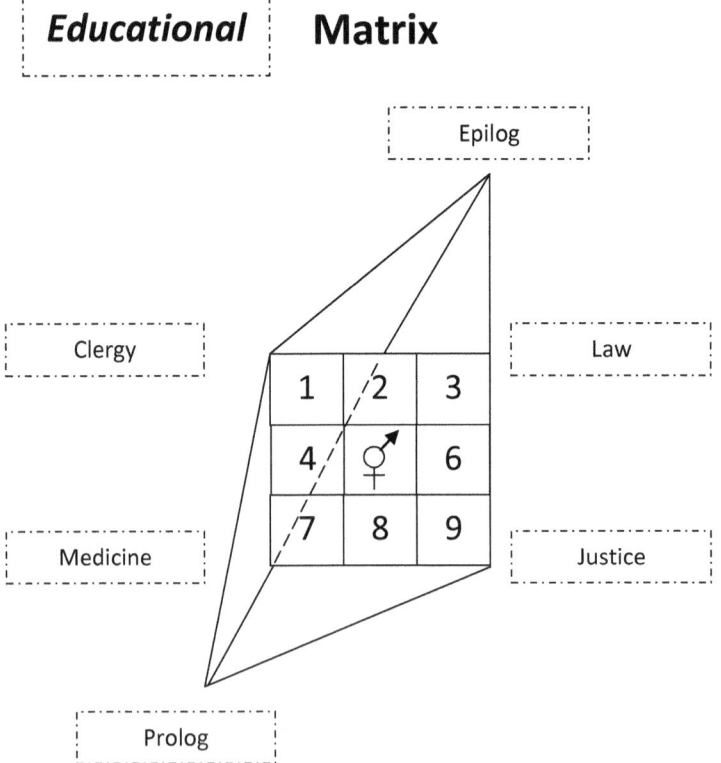

Epilog Sonnet

(14 steps to progress)

1. We are caught up in a statistical morass: a turmoil founded on the variability of language
2. How humans think is how we progress it cannot be done without the preservation of Health and the rule of Law
3. "Governance" for the people should constitutionally guarantee this right: does it not?
4. Strife and conflict has no place in Health
5. Health is created by Family jointed or disjointed
6. The product of the junction should warrant Health: government should protect it
7. Envisioning this future the learned professions Clergy, Medicine and Law hold the keys to the kingdom
8. Technical and financial progress will and must compliment this civil process
9. But humans must remember: the three species that stand erect on this planet are trees, humans and penguins: the polar definition of advanced life on earth
10. Further there is no "or" in Health the alternative is Disease
11. The bridge is risky and environment has control intermittent trauma is inevitable: preserve our Human Ethic
12. Logically people should control technical progress through communication and separate the food of Health from Environment
13. For Health Education is the only fixed guarantee plus the Art of Compromise: Question, Science and Politics
14. Humans are disgustingly healthy; support the Healthiest extremes: 1) children, 2) disabled and 3) elderly; add Ombudsman justice for the family at any cost! For freedoms sake let others choose their coarse.

Concept

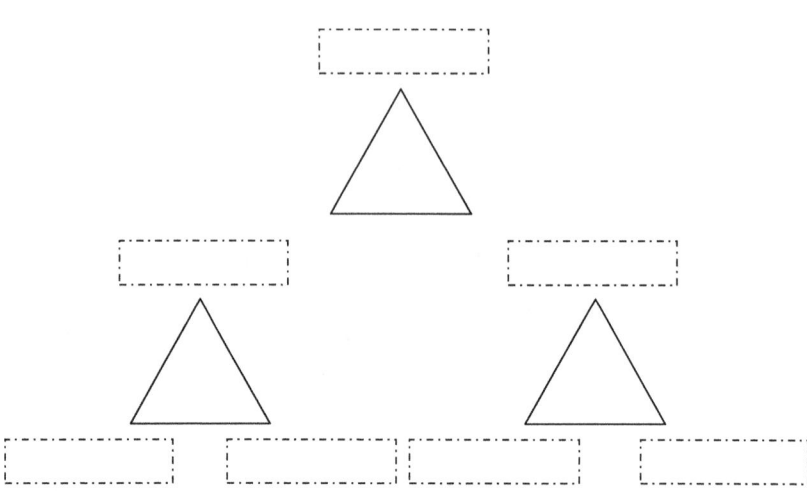

Matrix

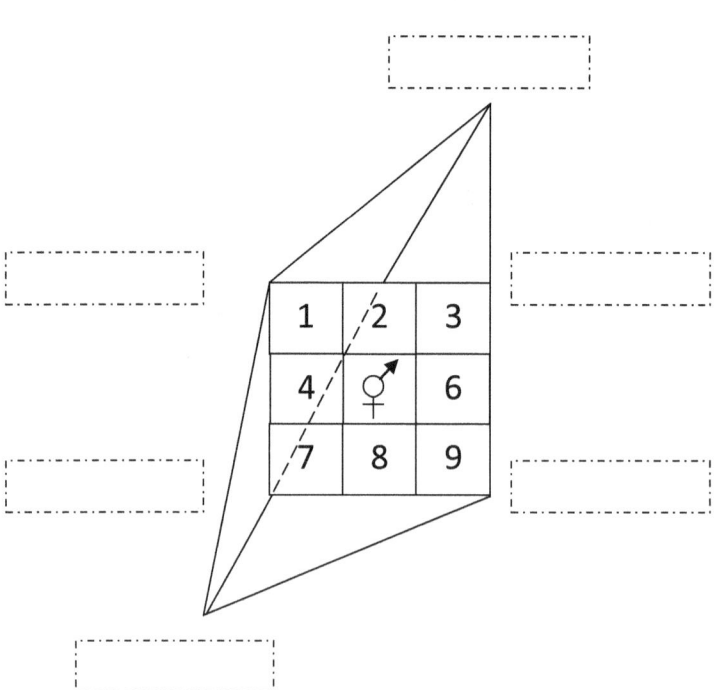

Keyword Index

The indexed words are taken from the graphic diagrams. Use them plus your own words to define concept words and polar words for the matrix diagrams. With polar words remember the antonym.

Word List

Notes

Notes

Notes

www.ingramcontent.com/pod-product-compliance
Lightning Source LLC
Chambersburg PA
CBHW060650290526
45793CB00001B/476